**ANIMALS**

**in the Wild**

First published in Belgium and Holland by Clavis Uitgeverij, Hasselt – Amsterdam, 2015
Copyright © 2015, Clavis Uitgeverij

English translation from the Dutch by Clavis Publishing Inc. New York
Copyright © 2016 for the English language edition: Clavis Publishing Inc. New York

Visit us on the web at www.clavisbooks.com

Animals in the Wild. The Bear written and illustrated by Renne
Original title: Wilde dieren in de natuur. De beer
Translated from the Dutch by Clavis Publishing

ISBN 978-1-60537-299-0

This book was printed in August 2016 at Publikum d.o.o., Slavka Rodica 6, Belgrade, Serbia

First Edition
10 9 8 7 6 5 4 3 2 1

Clavis Publishing supports the First Amendment and celebrates the right to read

# the
# BEAR

Renne

Clavis

**NEW YORK**

# WHERE DOES THE BEAR LIVE?

Deep in the forest and on the steep mountainsides
lives a wonderful wild animal: **the brown bear.**

This giant loves deserted areas.
He lives in places where rivers cleave the scenery,
where pines, oaks and birches reach into the sky
and raspberries and blackberries cover the mossy ground.

There are rocks, trees....
And look! There's a **cave**!

This bear has walked a long way.
Now it's time for a nap in the cave!

## WHAT DOES THE BEAR LOOK LIKE?

**The brown bear** is heavy and large.
He has strong paws and a tiny tail.
Nevertheless, this colossus can run
up to 30 miles an hour!

He can swim, climb
and clamber over large boulders.
Sometimes he stands on his hind legs
but if he walks,
he does so on his four paws.

The color of his thick,
long **fur** can go from
beige to black.

The bear is a **plantigrade** animal.
That means he walks
with his feet flat on the ground.

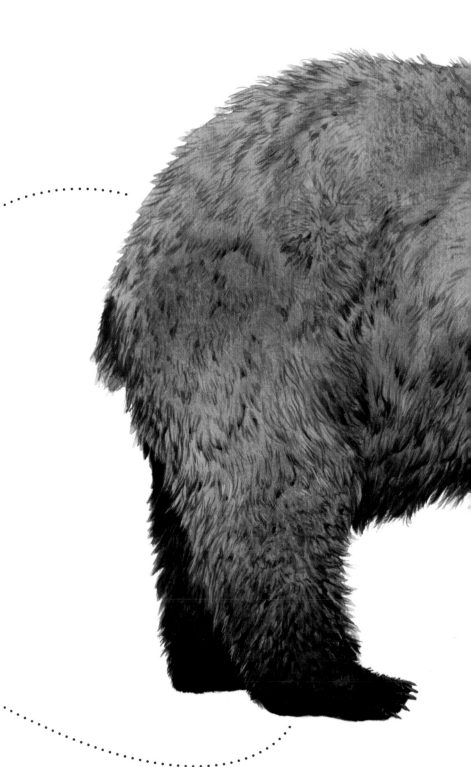

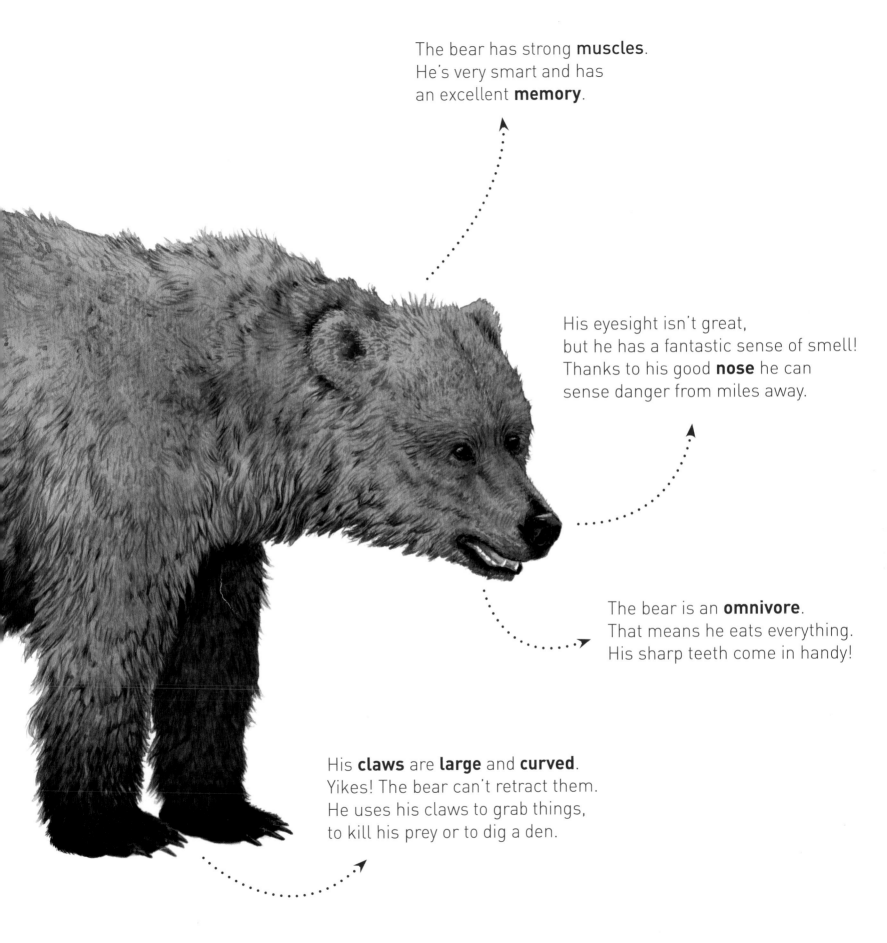

The bear has strong **muscles**. He's very smart and has an excellent **memory**.

His eyesight isn't great, but he has a fantastic sense of smell! Thanks to his good **nose** he can sense danger from miles away.

The bear is an **omnivore**. That means he eats everything. His sharp teeth come in handy!

His **claws** are **large** and **curved**. Yikes! The bear can't retract them. He uses his claws to grab things, to kill his prey or to dig a den.

# HOW DOES THE BEAR SPEND HIS DAY?

The bear goes out at night. He doesn't like people.
Only in uninhabited areas like Siberia
is he active during the daytime.

The bear has to wander a lot in order to find food.
He also needs water to cool down:
his thick fur makes the heat unbearable.

The bear loves open space. His territory covers at least twelve square miles.
Plantigrade mammals don't really defend their territory.
Sometimes two bears even live in the same area.

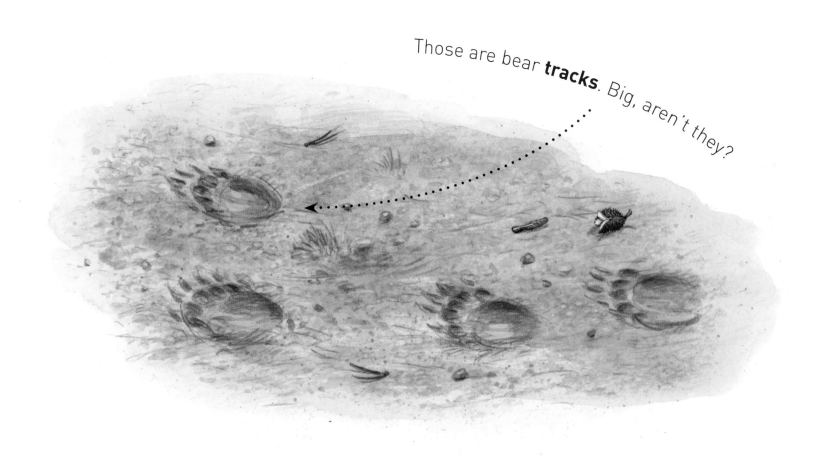

Those are bear **tracks**. Big, aren't they?

Ah, the water feels good!

# HOW DO BEARS GET ALONG?

The bear is a loner.
He doesn't seek the company of other bears.
In the summer, the male and female bear meet up
and stay together to have their young.
During the rest of the year, they live separately.

Mother bear looks after her cubs by herself. She's very brave.
She tries to avoid her own kind. You never know!

Sometimes several animals gather in a place
with a lot of food.
Then they all enjoy the bounty.
A fight is rare.

**What a catch!**
**Let's eat!**

My mom is very strong.
I like staying close to her.

## WHAT DOES THE BEAR EAT?

The bear is tremendously fond of good food.
He eats all kinds of things!
In the summer months he likes eating plants,
but he also catches animals.
With a swipe of his big paw, he can kill a young boar,
a deer or a mountain goat.

He lifts rocks to catch insects
and digs deep into the holes of rodents.
Those claws are useful!
The bear is also an excellent fisherman.
He catches fish that jump out of the water
or slings them onto the riverbank.

In the fall the bear
enjoys **wild fruit**.

Mm.... **Eggs** and **honey**!
Yummy!

This bear has caught something.
He's a good fisherman!

# WHAT'S THE BEAR'S SECRET?

Stroll around in the cold winter snow?
No, thank you! The bear sleeps from mid-December to mid-March.
He **hibernates**.
Hibernation is a very special and mysterious thing.
It's a clever trick to survive the hard winter.
The bear's body cools down, his heart beats more slowly and his breathing slows too.
Thanks to the fat reserves he built up in the fall,
he can survive a few months without eating anything!

The bear hibernates in a cave or a den
that he has dug in a mountain slope.
Inside, he makes a comfortable mattress
using a pile of grass and leaves.
The perfect spot to doze until spring!

**I found some nice, soft leaves.**
**I'm sure I can snore away on them for months.**

Do not disturb, please.
I'm hibernating!

# HOW DO BEAR CUBS COME INTO THE WORLD?

In summer, the male bear seeks a female. Often, he returns
to the same female for years. He courts her by softly biting her back.
Afterwards, they mate. The males often fight during this period,
but it rarely ends badly.
The female bear interrupts her winter sleep to give birth to her cubs.
If she's young, she has one cub. Later on, the number goes up to three.
The bear cub is very tiny at birth.
If he were bigger, his mom wouldn't have enough food for him.
After all, she's living off her own fat reserves.
Every now and then she wakes up from her winter sleep to feed her young.
All winter long, the cub stays close to his mother's warm fur.

He weighs no more than 0,9 pounds
and is no longer than 8 inches:
a **mini bear**!

These twins are growing up fast.
Soon they can go outside.
That will be fun!

# HOW DO BEAR CUBS GROW UP?

In spring, the sleepyheads leave their hiding-place.
The little ones can finally discover the outside world!
They play a lot in the first years. Mother bear teaches them
to climb trees, to fish and to hunt. If the cubs are naughty,
she gives them a cuff on the ear!
The next winter, the whole family crawls into the same den
to hibernate again.

The little bears become more independent every year.
They're fully grown by the age of three.
Then they all go their own way and start their own lives.

**Ouch! Ha ha!
Stop pushing me!**

What's hidden underneath this rock?
Mm, juicy insects!

# WHO ARE THE BEAR'S ENEMIES?

Wolves, lynxes, European wildcats and foxes
sometimes kill very young bears when they are alone in their den.
Unfortunately, this can happen when mother bear is out
looking for food in the spring, after hibernating.

A fully-grown bear has only one enemy: man.
Man has been hunting bears for centuries
to protect himself or his herds.

Today the Eurasian brown bear is protected,
but his habitat is threatened.
Therefore the bear, a wonderful wild animal, is in danger.

the wolf

the European wildcat

the lynx

the fox

Sometimes the bear is chased away by force.
That's why he doesn't like man....

## ONCE UPON A TIME...

Yikes! A bear walking upright is scary.
If he attacks, he looks like a monster!
For more than 40,000 years the bear has inspired
the imagination of man.
In the Middle Ages, he was displayed on many shields.
He symbolized power, nobility and courage.
He plays a part in fairy tales as well: the evil wizard
loves to turn the prince into a giant bear.
But who accompanies little children to their beds?
That's right: a teddy bear!

**Do you have a teddy bear as well?**

Geez! I wish the wizard had turned me into a bear instead of into a frog!

# THE BEAR FAMILY

The bear family (*ursidae*) includes seven species, spread over Europe, North and South America, Asia and even the Arctic.

**Brown bear:** Europe, North America, Asia
**Polar bear:** the Arctic
**Sloth bear:** Asia
**American black bear:** North America
**Sun bear or Malayan bear:** Asia
**Spectacled bear:** South America
**Asiatic black bear:** Asia

**Polar bear**
*(Thalarctos maritimus)*

**Brown bear**
*(Ursus arctos)*

**Sloth bear**
*(Melursus ursinus)*

**American black bear**
*(Euarctos americanus)*

**Spectacled bear** *(Tremarctos ornatus)*

**Sun bear or Malayan bear**
*(Helarctos malayanus)*

*Asiatic black bear*
*(Selenarctos thibetanus)*

# MORE FACTS ABOUT THE BROWN BEAR

**Class:** mammals
**Order:** predator
**Family:** bears
**Genus and species:** Ursus arctos
**Length:** 6,5 to 8 feet
**Weight:** 200 to 660 pounds,
depending on the region
**Habitat:** forests and mountains
**Diet:** omnivorous (plants, insects, honey,
birds, fish, lizards, frogs, small and bigger
mammals....)

**Lifestyle:** solitary, except during mating season
**Mating season:** spring – summer
**Gestation:** 7 to 8 months
**Birth of the bear cubs:** mid-January to
mid-February, during hibernation
**Litter:** 1 to 3 bear cubs, very rarely 4
**Sexually mature:** females at the age of 3,
males at the age of 4
**Life expectancy:** maximum 30 years

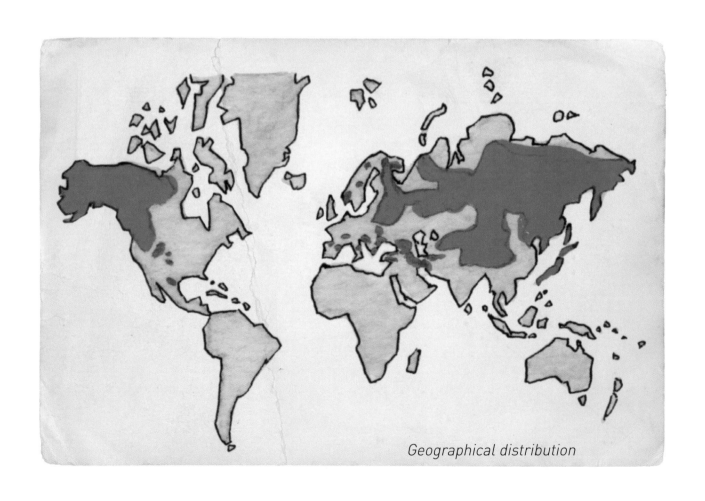

*Geographical distribution*

# NICE WORDS TO LEARN

- **HABITAT:**
  place where a certain species lives

- **PLANTIGRADE MAMMAL:**
  animal that walks with his feet flat on the ground

- **OMNIVORE:**
  animal that eats both plants and animals

- **TERRITORY:**
  area an animal occupies and defends

- **CONGENER:**
  animal of the same species

- **HIBERNATION:**
  a state of inactivity during winter, characterized by low body temperature

- **MATE:**
  to come together to make babies

- **MAMMALS:**
  animals who nurse their young

- **LITTER:**
  number of cubs an animal bears in one birth

- **LIFE EXPECTANCY:**
  normal duration of life